# SCHOLASTIC

# 10 MINUTE

# SATs TESTS

## GRAMMAR, PUNCTUATION AND SPELLING

AGES 6-7
YEAR 2

# KS1

Scholastic Education, an imprint of Scholastic Ltd

Book End, Range Road, Witney, Oxfordshire, OX29 0YD

Registered office: Westfield Road, Southam, Warwickshire CV47 0RA

www.scholastic.co.uk

© 2017, Scholastic Ltd

1 2 3 4 5 6 7 8 9 7 8 9 0 1 2 3 4 5 6

British Library Cataloguing-in-Publication Data

A catalogue record for this book is available from the British Library.

**ISBN 9781407176116**

Printed and bound in Great Britain by Bell and Bain Ltd, Glasgow

**Author**
Shelley Welsh

**Editorial**
Audrey Stokes, Kate Pedlar, Suzanne Adams

**Cover and Series Design**
Scholastic Design Team: Nicolle Thomas and Neil Salt

**Cover Illustration**
Adam Linley @ Beehive Illustration, Visual Generation @ Shutterstock

# Contents

# How to use this book

**This book contains ten different Grammar, Punctuation and Spelling tests for Year 2, each containing SATs-style questions. As a whole, the complete set of tests provides broad coverage of the test framework for this age group.**

It is intended that children will take around ten minutes to complete each part of each test (ten minutes for grammar and punctuation, and ten minutes for spelling); however, timings at this age are not strict, so allow your child as much time as they need.

## Grammar and punctuation tests

Each test comprises nine questions, which amount to 10 marks in total. Some questions require a selected response, where children choose the correct answer from a list. Other questions require a constructed response, where children insert a word or punctuation mark, or write a short answer of their own.

## Spelling tests

There are ten questions in each test which amount to 10 marks. Read each spelling number followed by *The word is...* Read the context sentence and then repeat *The word is...* Leave at least a 12-second gap between spellings. More information can be found on page 59.

The glossary on page 50 provides a useful guide to the grammatical terms that children need to be familiar with, as well as some terms that support a wider understanding of English grammar.

Marks

1. Circle the **two nouns** in the sentence below.

The porridge bubbled gently in the pan.

1

2. Write the missing **punctuation mark** at the end of the sentence below.

Are you coming to my party on Saturday ___

1

3. Look at where the arrow is pointing. Which **punctuation mark** is missing?

Last night, it started to snow Sami couldn't wait to go outside.
↑

Tick **one.**

a comma ☐

a question mark ☐

a full stop ☐

an apostrophe ☐

1

**10 MINS**

Marks

**4.** Circle the correct **verb** to complete this sentence.

Billy _____ his lunch hungrily.

Circle **one.**

| eated | eaten | ate |

1

**5.** Tick **one** box to show where a **comma** should go in the sentence below.

We saw zebras giraffes and elephants at the zoo.

↑    ↑    ↑         ↑

☐    ☐    ☐         ☐

1

**6.** What type of word is <u>softly</u> in the sentence below?

Mum sang <u>softly</u> to my baby brother.

Tick **one.**

an adjective ☐

a verb ☐

a noun ☐

an adverb ☐

KEEP IT GOING!

1

6

Marks

**7.** Match each word on the left to the correct **suffix** on the right. Each word should link to a different suffix.

One has been done for you.

| | |
|---|---|
| hurt | ness |
| strong | ful |
| good | er |
| hope ———————— | less |

1

**8.** Write **one** word to complete the sentence below in the **present tense**.

The bus _____ always late on Fridays.

1

**9.** Explain why the **two** underlined words in this sentence start with a **capital letter**.

<u>After</u> breakfast, <u>Sophie</u> went for a walk.

_____

_____

_____

2

7

Marks

1.  We had a lot of _____ in the park.

2.  Mum decided to _____ a pie.

3.  My favourite _____ is a horse.

4.  I asked Patrick to _____ our group.

5.  Our teacher told us to use a _____.

6.  Sami _____ about his trip to Scotland.

7.  The bull _____ across the field.

8.  We had to _____ for five hours to get home.

9.  My birthday was the _____ day of my life.

10. Mrs Smith read us a story about buried _____.

10

Well done! END OF TEST 1!

Marks

1. What type of word is underlined in the sentence below?

Mum covered the cake with some <u>smooth</u> icing.

**Tick one.**

an adverb ☐

an adjective ☐

a verb ☐

a noun ☐

1

2. Circle the **two nouns** in the sentence below.

My big brother ate all the pizza.

1

Marks

**3.** Match each pair of words on the left with its short form on the right.

One has been done for you.

| I have | they're |
| they are | you'll |
| we had | I've |
| you will | we'd |

1

**4.** Tick the sentence that is a **question**.

Tick **one.**

My friend Mia has asked me to her house. ☐

You have been to Scotland, haven't you? ☐

How tall you have grown! ☐

Insects have six legs and spiders have eight. ☐

1

KEEP IT GOING!

**10 MINS**

Marks

**5.** Add either <u>s</u> or <u>es</u> to make each word **plural.**
One has been done for you.

church<u>es</u>

chair _____

box _____

1

**6.** Add a **suffix** to the **verb** <u>wonder</u> to complete this sentence.

Joe wonder_____ whether it was time to open his presents.

1

**7.** Tick the sentence below that is a **statement.**

Tick **one.**

When do you go on holiday? ☐

Usually, we go on holiday in August. ☐

What an amazing time we had on holiday! ☐

Send me a postcard when you go on holiday. ☐

1

Marks

**8.** Tick to show whether each sentence is in the **present tense** or the **past tense**.

| Sentence | Present tense | Past tense |
|---|---|---|
| Mum was gardening all weekend. | | |
| Pippa is brushing her teeth. | | |
| The birds were singing in the trees. | | |

1

**9.** Why does each underlined word in the sentence have an **apostrophe**?

<u>I've</u> just found <u>Sami's</u> lunch box, which he lost yesterday.

_____

_____

_____

2

KEEP IT GOING!

10 MINS

Marks

1. The teacher put my book on the _____.

2. Dad went for a _____ in the park.

3. Ushma had to _____ to the invitation.

4. The referee kept the _____.

5. We have _____ our stories.

6. Rob left his _____ at the swimming pool.

7. I saw a _____ at the zoo.

8. It was a bit of a _____ in the back of the car.

9. We watched _____ last night.

10. The best _____ of the book was the middle.

10

Well done! END OF TEST 2!

**10 MINS**

Marks

**1.** Add a **punctuation mark** at the end of the sentence below to complete it.

Have you got any brothers or sisters ___

1

**2.** What type of word is underlined in the sentence below?

The old dog <u>limped</u> slowly home.

**Tick one.**

an adverb ☐

a noun ☐

an adjective ☐

a verb ☐

1

**3.** Tick the sentence that is an **exclamation**.

**Tick one.**

You look wonderful in your new coat. ☐

Put on your new coat, please. ☐

How wonderful you look in your new coat! ☐

Have you put on your new coat? ☐

1

Marks

4. Circle **two verbs** in the sentence below.

We were happy that our team won the race.

1

5. Tick the correct word to complete the sentence below.

I like going to the seaside _____ I enjoy swimming.

Tick **one.**

when ☐

if ☐

that ☐

because ☐

1

6. Tick the correct **suffix** that changes the word <u>hope</u> to an **adjective.**

Tick **one.**

est ☐

ment ☐

ful ☐

1

7. Write the missing **punctuation mark** at the end of this sentence to complete it.

What a great time we had ___

1

15

10 MINS

Marks

8. Read the sentences below. Tick the word that best describes the sentences.

> **Making Toast**
> 1. Put the bread in the toaster.
> 2. Wait for it to pop up.
> 3. Spread it with butter and eat it.

Tick **one.**

exclamations ☐

questions ☐

statements ☐

commands ☐

1

9. The arrows are pointing to verbs in the **past tense**. Write them in the **present tense** in the boxes.

One has been done for you.

| sing | |
|------|--|

↓                                              ↓

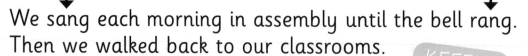

We sang each morning in assembly until the bell rang. Then we walked back to our classrooms.

↑

KEEP IT GOING!

2

Marks

1. Mum said she would _____ us when lunch was ready.

2. The bird _____ to its nest.

3. We wrote down the _____ that our teacher read out.

4. Mia was sad but Clara was _____.

5. Tammy always _____ to the teacher's questions.

6. Aisha does not _____ a pet.

7. The _____ on Tom's bike is broken.

8. We watched the _____ jump from tree to tree.

9. There is a shop in our _____.

10. Dad did a _____ trick at my party.

10

Well done! END OF TEST 3!

Marks

**1.** Tick the correct word to complete the sentence below.

We could have cake _____ we could have ice cream at Lucy's party.

Tick **one.**

when ☐

if ☐

so ☐

or ☐

1

**2.** Which sentence is a **command**?

Tick **one.**

What a terrible day it is! ☐

Come and sit down. ☐

Aren't you very tired? ☐

I've hurt my thumb. ☐

1

**3.** Add a **suffix** to the word <u>hang</u> to complete the sentence below.

As Mum was hang_____ the washing out, it began to rain.

1

Marks

4. Add a **suffix** to the word <u>tall</u> to complete the sentence below.

Jake is the tall_____ out of the ten boys in our class.

1

5. What type of word is underlined in the sentence below?

Ushma wrote her name <u>neatly</u> on the page.

Tick **one.**

an adjective ☐

a verb ☐

a noun ☐

an adverb ☐

1

**10 MINS**

Marks

**6. a.** Which sentence uses an **apostrophe** correctly?

Tick **one.**

My brothers books' were missing. ☐

My brother's books were missing. ☐

My brothers book's were missing. ☐

My brothers books were missing. ☐

1

**b.** What does the apostrophe in the correct sentence tell you? Why is it there?

_____

_____

_____

1

**7.** Add **one comma** to the sentence below.

We packed our swimming trunks towels and goggles for our trip to the pool.

1

KEEP IT GOING!

Marks

**8.** Add a suitable **adjective** to make a **noun phrase** from the words below.

my _____ sister

1

**9.** Circle the correct **verbs** so that the sentence is written in the **past tense**.

Dad **watches / watched** tennis on TV while Mum **played / plays** cricket with us in the garden.

1

Marks

1.  I _____ to learn my spellings every night.

2.  We followed the _____ through the woods.

3.  Our school uniform is _____ and grey.

4.  Our teacher let us _____ a film at the end of term.

5.  At the zoo, we saw a funny _____.

6.  Dev saw three _____ in the field.

7.  There are lots of _____ in the garden.

8.  Dad went to a _____ restaurant for his birthday.

9.  My uncle has just _____ his driving test.

10. Eve forgot to take her swimming _____ to school.

10

Well done! END OF TEST 4!

# Test 5

## Grammar and Punctuation

**10 MINS**

**1.** Write **one** word on the line below to complete the sentence in the **present tense**.

I always _____ my teeth after breakfast.

1

**2.** Tick the correct word to complete the sentence below.

_____ it rains, we will have to play indoors.

Because ☐

That ☐

If ☐

And ☐

1

**3.** Circle **two full stops** that are in the wrong places. One has been done for you.

After break, we went. into our classroom. Our teacher showed us. some interesting animal pictures. One was a picture of a lion. and one was a giraffe.

1

23

**10 MINS**

Marks

**4.** Write the words below in the correct order, to make a sentence.

| our plants | so they wouldn't | Mrs Smith |

| watered | die. |

_____

_____

1

**5.** Write the **plural** form of these nouns. Write the full word for each one.

Remember any spelling rules.

church _____

baby _____

1

**6.** Which sentence below is a **statement**?

Tick **one.**

Eat your ice cream before it melts! ☐

Maddie likes beans but not peas. ☐

Do you like pears or apples best? ☐

What an amazing day it's been! ☐

1

Marks

**7.** Circle **two nouns** in the sentence below.

All three dogs were lying on the rug.

1

**8.** Tick the correct sentence to show that Zac's jumping is happening now.

**Tick one.**

Zac is jumping on the trampoline. ☐

Zac will jump on the trampoline. ☐

Zac jumped on the trampoline. ☐

Zac was jumping on the trampoline! ☐

1

**9.** Joe and Zainab want to know more about insects.

Write a **question** they could ask their teacher.

Remember to punctuate your answer correctly.

_____

_____

2

Marks

1.  Ralph slammed the _____ as he left the room.

2.  It was a really _____ car.

3.  Our teacher collected the _____ for the class trip.

4.  Mum said she wouldn't go to that restaurant _____.

5.  Mia easily won the running _____.

6.  The _____ went over the river.

7.  I don't _____ all of my times tables.

8.  Mum said we should be careful near the _____.

9.  There were _____ flowers in the park.

10. Dad likes _____ in his tea.

10

Well done! END OF TEST 5!

**Marks**

1. Circle the **adjective** in the sentence below.

It was a sunny day so we went to the beach.

1

2. Tick the sentence below that is an **exclamation**.

Tick **one.**

Stop making such a mess. ☐

Why have you made such a mess? ☐

You have made a mess. ☐

What a mess you have made! ☐

1

3. What type of word is underlined in the sentence below?

The head teacher spoke <u>calmly</u> to the upset boy.

Tick **one.**

an adjective ☐

a verb ☐

an adverb ☐

a noun ☐

1

10
MINS

Marks

**4.** Which sentence uses an **apostrophe** correctly?

Tick **one.**

We didnt' want to go out in the rain. ☐

We didn't want to go out in the rain. ☐

We didnt wan't to go out in the rain. ☐

We did'nt want to go out in the rain. ☐

1

**5.** Add a **suffix** to the word <u>care</u> to complete the sentence below.

Jamie was very care_____ when he held the tiny baby.

1

Marks

6. How do you know that the sentence below is an exclamation? Give two reasons.

How beautiful that little puppy is!

_____

_____

_____

2

7. Tick one sentence that is correct.

Tick **one.**

Henry walked to the bus stop and gets on the bus. ☐

Henry walked to the bus stop and got on the bus. ☐

Henry walks to the bus stop and got on the bus. ☐

Henry is walking to the bus stop and got on the bus. ☐

1

**10 MINS**

Marks

**8.** Add an **adjective** between the words below to make a **noun phrase**.

the _____ apple

1

**9.** Tick to show whether each sentence is written in the **past** or **present tense**.

One has been done for you.

| Sentence | Present tense | Past tense |
|---|---|---|
| My favourite hobby is swimming. | | |
| I liked swimming in the sea on holiday. | | |
| There are no beaches near where I live. | | |

1

KEEP IT GOING!

Marks

1. The _____ bird pecked at the ground.

2. We threw the _____ to each other.

3. Johnny has football every _____.

4. There was a _____ spider in the bath.

5. We had to _____ up warm as it was very cold.

6. My picture was good but Freddy's was the _____.

7. There is _____ better than a warm, sunny day.

8. I need to _____ my handwriting.

9. We had to be _____ as the baby was asleep.

10. Dad had to _____ quietly upstairs with Mum's surprise present.

10

Well done! END OF TEST 6!

Marks

**1.** Which word completes the sentence below?

Last summer, we went to a swimming pool _____ had a water slide.

Tick **one.**

that ☐

or ☐

but ☐

because ☐

1

**2.** Complete the sentence below by adding a final **punctuation mark**.

How old are you __

1

**3.** Why do the underlined words in the sentence start with a **capital letter**?

Mum took <u>Archie</u> and me to <u>London</u> last weekend.

_____

_____

1

**4.** Circle **two verbs** in the sentence below.

We went to Scotland on holiday and visited many beautiful places.

1

Marks

**5.** What type of word is <u>bravely</u> in the sentence below?

The prince <u>bravely</u> defeated the angry dragon.

Tick **one.**

an adjective ☐

a verb ☐

a noun ☐

an adverb ☐

1

**6.** Look at where the arrow is pointing.

We brushed our teeth combed our hair and climbed into bed. ↑

What punctuation mark is missing?

Tick **one.**

a full stop ☐

an exclamation mark ☐

a comma ☐

an apostrophe ☐

1

Marks

**7.** Add <u>er</u> and <u>est</u> to each of the following adjectives.

One has been done for you.

| Adjective | <u>er</u> suffix | <u>est</u> suffix |
|---|---|---|
| pretty | prett**ier** | prett**iest** |
| tall | | |
| happy | | |

2

**8.** Which sentence is in the **past tense**?

Tick **one.**

My friend Tania, who gets the bus,
lives miles away from school. ☐

There were at least ten children
who arrived late when it snowed. ☐

We always walk to school when it snows. ☐

Our teacher says we are the
best singers in the school. ☐

1

**9.** Circle **two nouns** in the sentence below.

We built sandcastles when we went to the beach.

1

Marks

1. Sam has two _____ for his bike.

2. Maddie's mum bought her some new _____.

3. My baby brother won't stop _____.

4. The train went through a _____.

5. Nishwa had a sore _____.

6. I _____ the eggs with the flour and sugar.

7. Mum used the _____ to call Gran.

8. The _____ played with the girls.

9. The little _____ climbed up the hill.

10. The children packed _____ bags for the trip.

10

Well done! END OF TEST 7!

Marks

**1.** Tick the correct word to complete the sentence below.

As Mia was _____ round the corner, she met her best friend Chloe.

Tick **one.**

walked ☐

walking ☐

walks ☐

walk ☐

1

**2.** What type of word is underlined in the sentence below?

The boat sailed on the <u>rough</u> sea.

Tick **one.**

an adjective ☐

a verb ☐

a noun ☐

an adverb ☐

1

**10 MINS**

Marks

3. Write **one** word on the line below to complete the sentence in the **past tense**.

Harriet _____ her breakfast quickly.

1

4. Which punctuation mark should be added to the end of the sentence below to complete it?

I forgot to hand my homework in today

**Tick one.**

a full stop ☐

a comma ☐

a question mark ☐

an apostrophe ☐

1

Marks

**5.** Add **two** letters at the beginning of the word <u>cooked</u>, to show that the food **has not** been cooked.

The food was ___cooked.

1

**6.** Add a **suffix** to the word <u>enjoy</u> to complete the sentence below.

My mum gets so much enjoy_____ out of her garden.

1

**7.** What type of sentence is written below?

Hold my hand.

Tick **one.**

a question ☐
an exclamation ☐
a statement ☐
a command ☐

1

**8.** Tick to show whether each sentence is written in the **past** or **present tense**.

Marks

| Sentence | Present tense | Past tense |
|---|---|---|
| I went to Sam's birthday party last year. | | |
| My friend Sam is seven today. | | |
| Sam goes to my school. | | |

1

**9.** Which sentences use an **apostrophe** correctly?

Tick **two.**

It was time for Ali's surprise.

He couldn't wait to open his present.

His brother said h'ed take a photograph.

His mums friend's took one too.

2

Marks

1. Our teacher said we had _____ worked very hard.

2. Mike _____ the dog gently.

3. I wrote down the _____ answer.

4. We climbed a _____ tree in the garden.

5. The cat had hurt its _____.

6. I banged my _____ on the chair leg.

7. Freddy could be quite _____ with his belongings.

8. Some _____ are scared of dogs.

9. I told _____ they could come to my party.

10. We watched the _____ diving competition.

10

Well done! END OF TEST 8!

Marks

**1.** Circle **two verbs** in the sentence below.

Amelia wrote to her cousin and told her all about her holiday.

1

**2.** What type of word is underlined in the sentence below?

Christopher wrote his name <u>clearly</u> on the front of the book.

Tick **one.**

an adjective ☐

a verb ☐

an noun ☐

an adverb ☐

1

**3.** Which sentence is a **statement**?

Tick **one.**

Have you been to Scotland before? ☐

We went to Scotland last summer. ☐

What beautiful sights we saw in Scotland! ☐

Show me your pictures of Scotland. ☐

1

Marks

**4.** What punctuation mark should be added to the end of this sentence to complete it?

How lovely you look in that dress

Tick **one.**

a question ☐

a full stop ☐

a comma ☐

an exclamation mark ☐

1

**5.** Write **one** word below to complete the sentence so that it is in the **present tense**.

We always _____ to our grandparents' house at Christmas.

1

**6.** Tick the correct word to complete the sentence below.

Mum said we could play outside _____ we had to put our coats on first.

Tick **one.**

if ☐

after ☐

but ☐

when ☐

1

**10 MINS**

Marks

**7.** Add a new word beginning to <u>packed</u> so that the sentence tells you that the suitcase is **not** being packed.

Dad ____ packed his suitcase when he got home from his trip.

1

**8.** Circle the correct **verbs** so that the sentence is in the **past tense**.

Our teacher **was** / **is** pleased with us because we **tidied** / **tidy** up the classroom.

1

**9.** Archie and Brogan are learning about plants.

Write a **question** that they could ask their teacher.

Remember to use correct punctuation.

_____

_____

2

Marks

1.  I filled my _____ with water.

2.  Carla was much _____ when she had learned her spellings.

3.  Our teacher has a _____ new car.

4.  Alfie _____ his dog but it wouldn't come.

5.  We visited Gran in _____.

6.  A _____ lives in the desert.

7.  In winter, the trees are _____.

8.  Mum washed my dirty _____.

9.  I can write my name _____.

10. We have been learning about places around the _____.

Well done! END OF TEST 9!

10

Marks

**1.** Tick the correct word to complete the sentence below.

Mr Desphpande has marked the homework

_____ I handed in yesterday.

Tick **one.**

when ☐

that ☐

if ☐

and ☐

1

**2.** Tick the sentence below that is a **command**.

Tick **one.**

Are you going swimming tonight? ☐

Come swimming with me tonight! ☐

You are coming swimming tonight, aren't you? ☐

Swimming starts at 6 o'clock tonight. ☐

1

**3.** Circle the **three adjectives** in the sentence below.

The beautiful blue butterfly landed on the delicate flower.

1

Marks

**4.** What type of word is underlined in the sentence below?

We lined up in the <u>playground</u> when the fire alarm rang.

Tick **one.**

a noun ☐

an adjective ☐

a verb ☐

an adverb ☐

1

**5.** What type of sentence is written below?

What a brilliant painting you have done!

Tick **one.**

a statement ☐

a command ☐

an exclamation ☐

a question ☐

1

Marks

**6.** Why do the underlined words in the sentence below start with a **capital letter**?

My friend <u>Orla</u> went to <u>Wales</u> at the weekend.

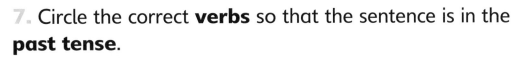

1

**7.** Circle the correct **verbs** so that the sentence is in the **past tense**.

After we **left** / **leave** the cinema, we **go** / **went** to a restaurant for pizza.

1

Marks

**8.** Tick **two** sentences that use an **apostrophe** correctly.

Tick **two.**

Its' time to go home soon.

Kieran's hat is not on his peg.

Wev'e got to hurry to get the bus.

Mum's going to be worried if we miss the bus.

2

**9.** Add the **suffix** <u>s</u> or <u>es</u> to each noun to make its **plural** form. You will need to add and take away letters.

baby        _____

fly        _____

1

Marks

1. I heard the bee _____ away.

2. The grass was _____ so we sat down for our picnic.

3. It was _____ for lunch.

4. The _____ rode a white horse.

5. Millie _____ hard to learn her times tables.

6. We learned what life was like in the _____.

7. Zainab spilled his drink of _____.

8. It was a long _____ up the hill.

9. The cake wasn't _____ cooked.

10. We were _____ practising for the school play.

10

Well done! END OF TEST 10!

# Grammar glossary

**adjective** – describes a noun, eg *blue dress*

**adverb** – describes the verb (*how something is done*), eg *she walked* **slowly**

**apostrophe** – used to show possession (Kieran's coat) or to replace missing letters in contractions
(do not ➝ don't; have not ➝ haven't)

**capital letter** – used at the beginning of a sentence, or for **proper nouns**

**comma** – used to separate items in a list, but not before *and* (they had sandwiches, crisps and fruit)

**command** – an instruction or order, to show what should or must be done

**co-ordinating conjunction** – a word used to connect two phrases of equal importance: *and, or, but*

**exclamation** – a phrase or sentence used to show heightened emotion, such as surprise, distress or excitement. Although statements and commands can also end in an exclamation mark, in the test only statements that start with 'What' or 'How' and end with an exclamation mark are accepted as exclamations.

**exclamation mark** – used at the end of an exclamation, or occasionally at the end of a command (!)

**full stop** – used at the end of a sentence (.)

**noun** – a 'thing', eg an object, place, person, idea, feeling

**noun phrase** – a pair or group of words that contains a noun and acts as the subject or object of a sentence, eg My **book** was…, the **blue book** was…, **the book on the table** was…

**object** (of a sentence/clause) – the object of the verb, or the thing that has something 'done' to it, eg The *dog* fetched **the bone**.

**prefix** – a group of letters that can be added to the beginning of the word to change its meaning, eg un*cooked*, **mis**heard

**proper noun** – the name of a person, place or organisatio

**question** – a sentence that asks something and usually requires an answer

**question mark** – used at the end of a question (?)

**root word** – a word in its shortest form, to which a prefix and/or suffix can be added, eg un*employment*, un**help**ful

**sentence** – a group of words that is complete in itself and begins with a capital letter and ends with a full stop; a sentence contains a subject and a verb

**simple past tense** – the form of the verb used to show that something has already happened, eg I **walked** home yesterday.

**simple present tense** – the form of the verb used to sho that something is happening now, or usually happens, eg I **walk** home *every day*; I **like** pizza.

**statement** – a phrase or sentence that gives information, eg *Glasgow is in Scotland; Jinc played football yesterday.*

**subject** (of a sentence/clause) – the thing that 'does' the verb, eg **The dog** fetched the bone.

**subordinate clause** – a phrase containing a subject and a verb, which is connected to another clause of greater importance and upon which it depends, eg I *wore my brown coat* **because it was my only one.**

**subordinating conjunction** – a word used to introduce subordinate clause, eg **when**, **if**, *because*, *that*

**suffix** – a group of letters that can be added to a word to change its meaning, eg help**ful**, slow**ly**

**verb** – a word that shows what someone is 'doing' or 'being', eg *go, swim, run, be, feel, think*

| Q | Mark scheme for Grammar and Punctuation Test 1 | Marks |
|---|---|---|
| 1 | **Award 1 mark** for two nouns correctly identified: porridge, pan. <br> **Grammar essentials:** Nouns are naming words for people, animals, objects ('porridge' and 'pan'), places, qualities, characteristics or emotions. | 1 |
| 2 | **Award 1 mark** for a question mark: Are you coming to my party on Saturday**?** <br> **Grammar/punctuation essentials:** A question is a type of sentence. It requires a question mark at the end. Some sentences end with a question tag: You're coming to my party on Saturday, aren't you? | 1 |
| 3 | **Award 1 mark** for: a full stop**.** <br> **Punctuation essentials:** Support your child by helping them see that the pause between 'snow' and 'Sami' is more than that afforded by a comma. The temptation is to insert a comma to create one sentence but a comma should not be used to connect two sentences. There are two sentences here, each with a subject and a verb. | 1 |
| 4 | **Award 1 mark** for: ate. <br> **Grammar essentials:** Children need to know the difference between the present and past tense so that their sentences make sense. There are many irregular verbs such as 'eat' ⟶ 'ate' that they just have to learn. | 1 |
| 5 | **Award 1 mark** for the correct box ticked (after 'zebras'): <br> We saw zebras**,** giraffes and elephants at the zoo. <br> **Punctuation essentials:** Remind children that in lists (like in this sentence), there is no comma before the word and. | 1 |
| 6 | **Award 1 mark** for: an adverb. <br> **Grammar essentials:** An adverb can say how something happens. Remember, not all adverbs end in 'ly' and not all words ending in 'ly' are adverbs. | 1 |
| 7 | **Award 1 mark** for all root words and suffixes matched correctly: hurtful, stronger, goodness. <br> **Grammar essentials:** A suffix is a letter or string of letters added to a word to turn it into another word. Sometimes, no change is needed to the spelling of the root word when the suffix is added. | 1 |
| 8 | **Award 1 mark** for: The bus **is** always late on Fridays. <br> **Grammar essentials:** Many children don't think of 'to be' as a verb as they don't see it as an action word. Verbs such as 'arrives' and 'comes' are not appropriate here as the adverb 'always' would need to come before them. | 1 |
| 9 | **Award 1 mark** for a reference to each of the following, up to a total of 2 marks: <br> 'After' is at the start of the sentence and a sentence always starts with a capital letter. <br> 'Sophie' is a name and a person's name always starts with a capital letter. <br> **Grammar essentials:** Remind children that names of towns, cities, countries, days of the week and months of the year also start with a capital letter. | 2 |
| | **Total** | 10 |

| Q | Mark scheme for Grammar and Punctuation Test 2 | Marks |
|---|---|---|
| 1 | **Award 1 mark** for: an adjective.<br>**Grammar essentials:** An adjective can come before a noun, to modify (describe) it, or after the verb 'be'. | 1 |
| 2 | **Award 1 mark** for both nouns circled: brother, pizza.<br>**Grammar essentials:** Nouns are naming words for people (brother), animals, objects (pizza), places, qualities, characteristics or emotions. | 1 |
| 3 | **Award 1 mark** for all words in the left column matched up with the correct contraction:<br><br>I have — they're<br>they are — you'll<br>we had — I've<br>you will — we'd<br><br>**Punctuation essentials:** The contracted form has an apostrophe just above where the missing letter or letters would be. | 1 |
| 4 | **Award 1 mark** for: You have been to Scotland, haven't you?<br>**Grammar essentials:** A question is a type of sentence. It requires a question mark at the end. Some sentences, like this one, end with a question tag: haven't you? | 1 |
| 5 | **Award 1 mark** for all endings correct: church**es**, chair**s**, box**es**.<br>**Grammar essentials:** Support the learning of plural forms of words ending in 'ch' and in 'x' by grouping similar words, eg church/churches; stitch/stitches; box/boxes; fox/foxes. | 1 |
| 6 | **Award 1 mark** for: wonder**ed**.<br>**Grammar essentials:** A suffix is a letter or string of letters added to the end of a word to make it into another word. The spelling of the root word of some verbs does not change when a suffix is added. For example: walk**s**, walk**ed**, walk**ing**. | 1 |
| 7 | **Award 1 mark** for: Usually, we go on holiday in August.<br>**Grammar essentials:** A statement is a type of sentence. It tells you something/gives information about something. | 1 |
| 8 | **Award 1 mark** for all sentences matched to the correct tense:<br><br><table><tr><td>Sentence</td><td>Present tense</td><td>Past tense</td></tr><tr><td>Mum was gardening all weekend.</td><td></td><td>√</td></tr><tr><td>Pippa is brushing her teeth.</td><td>√</td><td></td></tr><tr><td>The birds were singing in the trees.</td><td></td><td>√</td></tr></table><br>**Grammar essentials:** 'Mum was gardening'... and 'The birds were singing'... are in the past progressive tense; 'Pippa is brushing'... is in the present progressive tense. They show actions in progress. | 1 |
| 9 | **Award 1 mark** for reference to each of the following:<br>'I've' has an apostrophe to show that the letters ha in have have been left out.<br>'Sami's' has an apostrophe to show that the lunchbox belongs to Sami.<br>**Punctuation essentials:** The apostrophe in contractions should be positioned exactly above where the missing letter or letters should be. The apostrophe to show possession should be positioned between the final letter of the noun and the letter 's'. In both cases, the height of the apostrophe should be the same as an ascender. | 2 |
| | **Total** | 10 |

| Q | Mark scheme for Grammar and Punctuation Test 3 | Marks |
|---|---|---|
| 1 | **Award 1 mark** for: Have you got any brothers or sisters?<br>**Punctuation essentials:** A question is always followed by a question mark. Ensure it is correctly orientated. | 1 |

| Q | Mark scheme for Grammar and Punctuation Test 3 | Marks |
|---|---|---|
| 2 | **Award 1 mark** for: a verb. <br> **Grammar essentials:** A verb is a doing or being word. | 1 |
| 3 | **Award 1 mark** for: How wonderful you look in your new coat! <br> **Grammar/punctuation essentials:** An exclamation sentence starts with 'How' or 'What' and contains a subject and a verb. It always ends with an exclamation mark. | 1 |
| 4 | **Award 1 mark** for both verbs circled: were, won. <br> **Grammar essentials:** Children often do not see 'to be' as a verb. Remember, a verb is a doing or a 'being' word. | 1 |
| 5 | **Award 1 mark** for: because. <br> **Grammar essentials:** 'because' is a subordinating conjunction giving a reason why. | 1 |
| 6 | **Award 1 mark** for: hope**ful**. <br> **Grammar essentials:** None of the other suffixes can be added to the word hope. | 1 |
| 7 | **Award 1 mark** for: What a great time we had**!** <br> **Grammar/punctuation essentials:** An exclamation sentence starts with 'How' or 'What' and contains a subject and a verb. It always ends with an exclamation mark. | 1 |
| 8 | **Award 1 mark** for: commands. <br> **Grammar essentials:** A command sentence tells you to do something. It contains a command (or imperative) verb. Instructions and recipes contain commands. | 1 |
| 9 | **Award 1 mark** for each verb in the correct form: rings, walk. <br> **Grammar essentials:** The present tense indicates something that is happening now or generally happens. | 2 |
| | **Total** | 10 |

| Q | Mark scheme for Grammar and Punctuation Test 4 | Marks |
|---|---|---|
| 1 | **Award 1 mark** for: or. <br> **Grammar essentials:** 'or' is a co-ordinating conjunction – there is equal importance given to the clauses or phrases that it links. | 1 |
| 2 | **Award 1 mark** for: Come and sit down. <br> **Grammar essentials:** A command sentence tells you to do something. It contains a command (or imperative) verb(s) ('come' and 'sit'). Instructions and recipes contain commands. | 1 |
| 3 | **Award 1 mark** for: hang**ing**. <br> **Grammar essentials:** A suffix is a letter or string of letters added to the end of a word to make it into another word. Sometimes, no change is needed to the spelling of the root word. | 1 |
| 4 | **Award 1 mark** for: tall**est**. <br> **Grammar essentials:** A suffix is a letter or string of letters added to the end of a word to make it into another word. Sometimes, no change is needed to the spelling of the root word. | 1 |
| 5 | **Award 1 mark** for: an adverb <br> **Grammar essentials:** Many adjectives can be turned into adverbs by adding the suffix 'ly'. An adverb describes how something is done. | 1 |
| 6 | **Award 1 mark** for: My brother's books were missing. <br> Award an additional mark for an explanation such as: It shows that the books belong to my brother. <br> **Punctuation essentials:** Here, the apostrophe indicates possession – the books 'belonging to' my brother. | 2 |
| 7 | **Award 1 mark** for a comma after 'trunks'. <br> **Punctuation essentials:** Remind children that in lists (like this sentence), there is no comma before the word 'and'. | 1 |
| 8 | **Award 1 mark** for any suitable adjective, such as: little, big, naughty. <br> **Grammar essentials:** A noun phrase contains a noun and additional words to modify (describe) it. | 1 |
| 9 | **Award 1 mark** for both verbs in the correct tense: watched, played <br> **Grammar essentials:** The past tense indicates a completed action. | 1 |
| | **Total** | 10 |

| Q | Mark scheme for Grammar and Punctuation Test 5 | Marks |
|---|---|---|
| 1 | **Award 1 mark** for any appropriate verb in the present tense, such as: brush, clean.<br>**Grammar essentials:** The present tense indicates something that is happening now or, as in this example, usually/regularly happens. | 1 |
| 2 | **Award 1 mark** for: If.<br>**Grammar essentials:** 'If' is a subordinating conjunction introducing a subordinate clause. | 1 |
| 3 | **Award 1 mark** for circling all the incorrectly placed full stops:<br>After break, we went. into our classroom. Our teacher showed us. some interesting animal pictures. One was a picture of a lion. and one was a giraffe.<br>**Punctuation essentials:** Remind children that a full stop comes at the end of a sentence. It helps to read the sentences out loud and to listen for 'natural' pauses. The letter after a full stop should be a capital letter as it is the start of a new sentence. | 1 |
| 4 | **Award 1 mark** for: Mrs Smith watered our plants so they wouldn't die.<br>**Punctuation essentials:** Ensure capital letters are used for Mrs Smith and that there is a final full stop. Accept minor copying errors. | 1 |
| 5 | **Award 1 mark** for the correct plural forms for both words: churches, babies.<br>**Grammar essentials:** Remind children of the 'y' ⟶ 'ies' spelling rule. | 1 |
| 6 | **Award 1 mark** for: Maddie likes beans but not peas.<br>**Grammar essentials:** A statement is a type of sentence. It tells you something/gives information about something. | 1 |
| 7 | **Award 1 mark** for both nouns circled: dogs, rug.<br>**Grammar essentials:** Nouns are naming words for people, animals (dogs), objects (rugs), places, qualities, characteristics or emotions. | 1 |
| 8 | **Award 1 mark** for: Zac is jumping on the trampoline.<br>**Grammar essentials:** is jumping is an example of the present progressive tense, which indicates an action in progress. | 1 |
| 9 | **Award 2 marks** for any appropriate question that starts with a capital letter and ends in a full stop.<br>**Award 1 mark** for an appropriate answer that starts with a capital letter but where the question mark is missing.<br>**Award 1 mark** for an appropriate answer that does not start with a capital letter but ends with a question mark.<br>For example:<br>  How many legs does an insect have? (2 marks)<br>  Why aren't spiders insects. (1 mark)<br>  are ladybirds insects? (1 mark)<br>**Grammar/punctuation essentials:** A question always starts with a capital letter (unless it follows a colon) and ends with a question mark. | 2 |
| | **Total** | 10 |

| Q | Mark scheme for Grammar and Punctuation Test 6 | Marks |
|---|---|---|
| 1 | **Award 1 mark** for: sunny.<br>**Grammar essentials:** An adjective can come before a noun, to modify (describe) it, or after the verb 'be'. | 1 |
| 2 | **Award 1 mark** for: What a mess you have made!<br>**Grammar essentials:** An exclamation sentence starts with 'How' or 'What' and contains a subject and a verb. It always ends with an exclamation mark. | 1 |
| 3 | **Award 1 mark** for: an adverb.<br>**Grammar essentials:** Many adjectives can be turned into adverbs by adding the suffix 'ly'. An adverb describes how something is done. | 1 |

| Q | Mark scheme for Grammar and Punctuation Test 3 | Marks |
|---|---|---|
| 4 | **Award 1 mark** for: We didn't want to go out in the rain.<br>**Punctuation essentials:** Here, the apostrophe indicates the omitted 'o' from the word 'not'. Ensure it is positioned and orientated correctly. | 1 |
| 5 | **Award 1 mark** for: care**ful** or care**less**.<br>**Grammar essentials:** A suffix is a letter or string of letters added to the end of a word to make it into another word. Sometimes, no change is needed to the spelling of the root word. | 1 |
| 6 | **Award 1 mark** for: It begins with 'How'.<br>**Award 1 mark** for: It ends with an exclamation mark.<br>**Grammar/punctuation essentials:** An exclamation sentence starts with 'How' or 'What' and contains a subject and a verb. It always ends with an exclamation mark. | 2 |
| 7 | **Award 1 mark** for: Henry walked to the bus stop and got on the bus.<br>**Grammar essentials:** Children need to be consistent in their choice of verb tenses. | 1 |
| 8 | **Award 1 mark** for any suitable adjective, such as: rosy, red, crunchy, delicious.<br>**Grammar essentials:** A noun phrase contains a noun and additional words to modify (describe) it. | 1 |
| 9 | **Award 1 mark** for all sentences matched to the correct tense.<br><br>| Sentence | Present tense | Past tense |<br>|---|---|---|<br>| My favourite hobby is swimming. | √ | |<br>| I liked swimming in the sea on holiday. | | √ |<br>| There are no beaches near where I live. | √ | |<br><br>**Grammar essentials:** The present tense indicates something that is happening now or generally happens. The past tense indicates a completed action. | 1 |
| | **Total** | **10** |

| Q | Mark scheme for Grammar and Punctuation Test 7 | Marks |
|---|---|---|
| 1 | **Award 1 mark** for: that.<br>**Grammar essentials:** 'that' is a subordinating conjunction introducing a subordinate clause. | 1 |
| 2 | **Award 1 mark** for: How old are you?<br>**Punctuation essentials:** A question is always followed by a question mark. Ensure the question mark is correctly orientated. | 1 |
| 3 | **Award 1 mark** for an answer that states that 'Archie' and 'London' are names (of a person/a place), proper nouns or naming words for people/places.<br>**Punctuation essentials:** A capital letter is always used at the beginning of a proper noun. | 1 |
| 4 | **Award 1 mark** for both verbs circled: went, visited.<br>**Grammar essentials:** A verb is a doing or being word. | 1 |
| 5 | **Award 1 mark** for: an adverb.<br>**Grammar essentials:** An adverb can say how something happens. Remember, not all adverbs end in 'ly' and not all words ending in 'ly' are adverbs. | 1 |
| 6 | **Award 1 mark** for: a comma.<br>**Punctuation essentials:** Remind children that in lists (like this sentence), there is no comma before the word 'and'. | 1 |
| 7 | **Award 1 mark** for: 'taller' and 'tallest'.<br>**Award 1 mark** for: 'happier' and 'happiest'.<br>**Grammar essentials:** A suffix is a letter or string of letters added to the end of a word to make it into another word. When adding the suffix 'er' or 'est' to a root word ending in 'y' with a consonant before it, the 'y' is changed to 'i'. | 2 |

| 8 | **Award 1 mark** for: There were at least ten children who arrived late when it snowed.<br>**Grammar essentials:** The past tense indicates a completed action. | 1 |
|---|---|---|
| 9 | **Award 1 mark** for both nouns circled: sandcastles, beach.<br>**Grammar essentials:** Nouns are naming words for people, animals, objects (sandcastles), places (beach), qualities, characteristics or emotions. | 1 |
| | **Total** | 10 |

| Q | Mark scheme for Grammar and Punctuation Test 8 | Marks |
|---|---|---|
| 1 | **Award 1 mark** for: walking.<br>**Grammar essentials:** 'was walking' is the past progressive tense, which shows a continuous action that was happening in the past. | 1 |
| 2 | **Award 1 mark** for: an adjective.<br>**Grammar essentials:** An adjective can come before a noun, to modify (describe) it, or after the verb 'be'. | 1 |
| 3 | **Award 1 mark** for an appropriate verb in the past tense, such as: ate.<br>**Grammar essentials:** The past tense indicates a completed action. Don't accept 'was eating' as the question asks for only one word. | 1 |
| 4 | **Award 1 mark** for: a full stop.<br>**Punctuation essentials:** The sentence is a statement and therefore ends in a full stop. | 1 |
| 5 | **Award 1 mark** for: **un**cooked.<br>**Grammar essentials:** A prefix (or word beginning) does not alter the spelling of the word it is joined to. | 1 |
| 6 | **Award 1 mark** for: enjoy**ment**.<br>**Grammar essentials:** Some nouns can be formed from verbs without any change to the spelling of the root word. | 1 |
| 7 | **Award 1 mark** for: a command.<br>**Grammar essentials:** A command sentence tells you to do something. It contains a command (or imperative) verb(s) (hold). Instructions and recipes contain commands. | 1 |
| 8 | **Award 1 mark** for: all sentences matched to the correct tense:<br><br>| Sentence | Present tense | Past tense |<br>|---|---|---|<br>| I went to Sam's birthday party last year. | | √ |<br>| My friend Sam is seven today. | √ | |<br>| Sam goes to my school. | √ | |<br><br>**Grammar essentials:** The present tense indicates something that is happening now or generally happens. It can also be a state of being, for example: Sam is seven today. The past tense indicates a completed action. | 1 |
| 9 | **Award 1 mark** for each correct sentence:<br>It was time for Ali's surprise.<br>He couldn't wait to open his present.<br>**Punctuation essentials:** In the first sentence, the apostrophe indicates possession; in the second sentence, the apostrophe indicates the omitted letter from 'not'. | 2 |
| | **Total** | 10 |

| Q | Mark scheme for Grammar and Punctuation Test 9 | Marks |
|---|---|---|
| 1 | **Award 1 mark** for both past-tense verbs circled: wrote, told.<br>**Grammar essentials:** The past tense indicates a completed action. | 1 |
| 2 | **Award 1 mark** for: an adverb.<br>**Grammar essentials:** An adverb can say how something happens. Remember, not all adverbs end in 'ly' and not all words ending in 'ly' are adverbs. | 1 |
| 3 | **Award 1 mark** for: We went to Scotland last summer.<br>**Grammar essentials:** A statement is a type of sentence. It tells you something/gives information about something. | 1 |
| 4 | **Award 1 mark** for: an exclamation mark.<br>**Grammar/punctuation essentials:** An exclamation sentence starts with 'How' or 'What' and contains a subject and a verb. It always ends with an exclamation mark. | 1 |
| 5 | **Award 1 mark** for a suitable verb in the present tense, such as: go, drive, travel.<br>**Grammar essentials:** The present tense indicates something that is happening now or generally happens. | 1 |
| 6 | **Award 1 mark** for: but.<br>**Grammar essentials:** but is a co-ordinating conjunction. There is equal importance given to the clauses or phrases that it links. | 1 |
| 7 | **Award 1 mark** for: **un**packed.<br>**Grammar essentials:** A prefix (or word beginning) is a letter string added to the beginning of a word, changing its meaning. The prefix does not change the spelling of the root word. | 1 |
| 8 | **Award 1 mark** for both past-tense verbs circled: was, tidied.<br>**Grammar essentials:** The past tense indicates a completed action. | 1 |
| 9 | **Award 2 marks** for an appropriate question that starts with a capital letter and ends in a full stop.<br>**Award 1 mark** for an appropriate answer that starts with a capital letter but where the question mark is missing.<br>**Award 1 mark** for an appropriate answer that does not start with a capital letter but ends with a question mark. For example:<br>◦ How do plants drink water? (2 marks)<br>◦ Can plants think. (1 mark)<br>◦ are mushrooms plants? (1 mark)<br>**Grammar/punctuation essentials:** A question always starts with a capital letter (unless it follows a colon) and ends with a question mark. | 2 |
| | **Total** | **10** |

| Q | Mark scheme for Grammar and Punctuation Test 10 | Marks |
|---|---|---|
| 1 | **Award 1 mark** for: that.<br>**Grammar essentials:** 'that' is a subordinating conjunction introducing a subordinate clause. | 1 |
| 2 | **Award 1 mark** for: Come swimming with me tonight!<br>**Grammar essentials:** A command sentence tells you to do something. It contains a command (or imperative) verb(s) (come). Instructions and recipes contain commands. | 1 |
| 3 | **Award 1 mark** for all three adjectives circled: beautiful, blue, delicate.<br>**Grammar essentials:** An adjective can come before a noun, to modify (describe) it, or after the verb 'be'. | 1 |
| 4 | **Award 1 mark** for: a noun.<br>**Grammar essentials:** Nouns are naming words for people, animals, objects, places (playground), qualities, characteristics or emotions. | 1 |
| 5 | **Award 1 mark** for: an exclamation.<br>**Grammar/punctuation essentials:** An exclamation sentence starts with 'How' or 'What' and contains a subject and a verb. It always ends with an exclamation mark. | 1 |
| 6 | **Award 1 mark** for an answer that states that 'Orla' and 'Wales' are names (of a person / a place). Also accept: These words are proper nouns, or naming words for people / places.<br>**Punctuation essentials:** A capital letter is always used at the beginning of a proper noun. | 1 |
| 7 | **Award 1 mark** for the correct form of both verbs circled: left, went.<br>**Grammar essentials:** The past tense indicates a completed action. | 1 |
| 8 | **Award 1 mark** for each correct sentence ticked:<br>Kieran's hat is not on his peg.<br>Mum's going to be worried if we miss the bus.<br>**Grammar essentials:** The apostrophe in the first sentence indicates possession – the hat belonging to Kieran. The apostrophe in the second sentence indicates the omitted letter 'i' in is. | 2 |
| 9 | **Award 1 mark** for both plural endings correct: babies, flies.<br>**Grammar essentials:** A suffix is a letter or string of letters added to the end of a word to make it into another word. When adding the suffix 'es' to a root word ending in 'y' with a consonant before it, the 'y' is changed to 'i'. | 1 |
| | **Total** | 10 |

# How to administer the spelling tests

There are ten short spelling tests in this book. Each test consists of ten questions; you should allow your child as much time as they need to complete them.

Read the instructions in the box below. The instructions are similar to the ones given in the National Curriculum tests. This will familiarise children with the style and format of the tests and show them what to expect.

*Listen carefully to the instructions I am going to give you.*

*I am going to read ten sentences to you. Each sentence on your answer sheet has a missing word. Listen carefully to the missing word and write it in the space provided, making sure you spell the word correctly.*

*I will read the word, then the word within the sentence, then repeat the word a third time.*

*Do you have any questions?*

Read the spellings as follows:

- Give the question number, 'Spelling 1'.
- Say, 'The word is...'
- Read the whole sentence to show the word in context.
- Repeat, 'The word is...'

Leave at least a 12-second gap between each spelling.

Then say, 'This is the end of the test. Please put down your pencil or pen.'

Each correct answer should be awarded **1 mark**.

# Spelling test transcripts

## Spelling test 1

**Spelling 1:** The word is **fun**.
We had a lot of **fun** in the park.
The word is **fun**.

**Spelling 2:** The word is **cook**.
Mum decided to **cook** a pie.
The word is **cook**.

**Spelling 3:** The word is **animal**.
My favourite **animal** is a horse.
The word is **animal**.

**Spelling 4:** The word is **join**.
I asked Patrick to **join** our group.
The word is **join**.

**Spelling 5:** The word is **pencil**.
Our teacher told us to use a **pencil**.
The word is **pencil**.

**Spelling 6:** The word is **talked**.
Sami **talked** about his trip to Scotland.
The word is **talked**.

**Spelling 7:** The word is **charged**.
The bull **charged** across the field.
The word is **charged**.

**Spelling 8:** The word is **travel**.
We had to **travel** for five hours to
get home.
The word is **travel**.

**Spelling 9:** The word is **happiest**.
My birthday was the **happiest** day of
my life.
The word is **happiest**.

**Spelling 10:** The word is **treasure**.
Mrs Smith read us a story about buried
**treasure**.
The word is **treasure**.

## Spelling test 2

**Spelling 1:** The word is **table**.
The teacher put my book on the **table**.
The word is **table**.

**Spelling 2:** The word is **jog**.
Dad went for a **jog** in the park.
The word is **jog**.

**Spelling 3:** The word is **reply**.
Ushma had to **reply** to the invitation.
The word is **reply**.

**Spelling 4:** The word is **score**.
The referee kept the **score**.
The word is **score**.

**Spelling 5:** The word is **written**.
We have **written** our stories.
The word is **written**.

**Spelling 6:** The word is **towel**.
Rob left his **towel** at the swimming pool.
The word is **towel**.

**Spelling 7:** The word is **giraffe**.
I saw a **giraffe** at the zoo.
The word is **giraffe**.

**Spelling 8:** The word is **squash**.
It was a bit of a **squash** in the back of
the car.
The word is **squash**.

**Spelling 9:** The word is **television**.
We watched **television** last night.
The word is **television**.

**Spelling 10:** The word is **section**.
The best **section** of the book was the
middle.
The word is **section**.

## Spelling test 3

**Spelling 1:** The word is **call**.
Mum said she would **call** us when lunch
was ready.
The word is **call**.

**Spelling 2:** The word is **flew**.
The bird **flew** to its nest.
The word is **flew**.

**Spelling 3:** The word is **word**.
We wrote down the **word** that our
teacher read out.
The word is **word**.

**Spelling 4:** The word is **sadder**.
Mia was sad but Clara was **sadder**.
The word is **sadder**.

**Spelling 5:** The word is **replies**.
Tammy always **replies** to the teacher's
questions.
The word is **replies**.

**Spelling 6:** The word is **have**.
Aisha does not **have** a pet.
The word is **have**.

**Spelling 7:** The word is **pedal**.
The **pedal** on Tom's bike is broken.
The word is **pedal**.

**Spelling 8:** The word is **squirrel**.
We watched the **squirrel** jump from tree
to tree.
The word is **squirrel**.

**Spelling 9:** The word is **village**.
There is a shop in our **village**.
The word is **village**.

**Spelling 10:** The word is **magic**.
Dad did a **magic** trick at my party.
The word is **magic**.

## Spelling test 4

**Spelling 1:** The word is **try**.
I **try** to learn my spellings every night.
The word is **try**.

**Spelling 2:** The word is **track**.
We followed the **track** through the
woods.
The word is **track**.

**Spelling 3:** The word is **blue**.
Our school uniform is **blue** and grey.
The word is **blue**.

**Spelling 4:** The word is **watch**.
Our teacher let us **watch** a film at the
end of term.
The word is **watch**.

**Spelling 5:** The word is **monkey**.
At the zoo, we saw a funny **monkey**.
The word is **monkey**.

**Spelling 6:** The word is **foxes**.
Dev saw three **foxes** in the field.
The word is **foxes**.

**Spelling 7:** The word is **flies**.
There are lots of **flies** in the garden.
The word is **flies**.

**Spelling 8:** The word is **fancy**.
Dad went to a **fancy** restaurant for his
birthday.
The word is **fancy**.

# Spelling test transcripts

**Spelling 9:** The word is **passed**.
My uncle has just **passed** his driving test.
The word is **passed**.

**Spelling 10:** The word is **kit**.
Eve forgot to take her swimming **kit** to school.
The word is **kit**.

## Spelling test 5

**Spelling 1:** The word is **door**.
Ralph slammed the **door** as he left the room.
The word is **door**.

**Spelling 2:** The word is **fast**.
It was a really **fast** car.
The word is **fast**.

**Spelling 3:** The word is **money**.
Our teacher collected the **money** for the class trip.
The word is **money**.

**Spelling 4:** The word is **again**.
Mum said she wouldn't go to that restaurant **again**.
The word is **again**.

**Spelling 5:** The word is **race**.
Mia easily won the running **race**.
The word is **race**.

**Spelling 6:** The word is **bridge**.
The **bridge** went over the river.
The word is **bridge**.

**Spelling 7:** The word is **know**.
I don't **know** all of my times tables.
The word is **know**.

**Spelling 8:** The word is **road**.
Mum said we should be careful near the **road**.
The word is **road**.

**Spelling 9:** The word is **beautiful**.
There were **beautiful** flowers in the park.
The word is **beautiful**.

**Spelling 10:** The word is **sugar**.
Dad likes **sugar** in his tea.
The word is **sugar**.

## Spelling test 6

**Spelling 1:** The word is **little**.
The **little** bird pecked at the ground.
The word is **little**.

**Spelling 2:** The word is **ball**.
We threw the **ball** to each other.
The word is **ball**.

**Spelling 3:** The word is **Tuesday**.
Johnny has football every **Tuesday**.
The word is **Tuesday**.

**Spelling 4:** The word is **giant**.
There was a **giant** spider in the bath.
The word is **giant**.

**Spelling 5:** The word is **wrap**.
We had to **wrap** up warm as it was very cold.
The word is **wrap**.

**Spelling 6:** The word is **nicest**.
My picture was good but Freddy's was the **nicest**.
The word is **nicest**.

**Spelling 7:** The word is **nothing**.
There is **nothing** better than a warm, sunny day.
The word is **nothing**.

**Spelling 8:** The word is **improve**.
I need to **improve** my handwriting.
The word is **improve**.

**Spelling 9:** The word is **quiet**.
We had to be **quiet** as the baby was asleep.
The word is **quiet**.

**Spelling 10:** The word is **tread**.
Dad had to **tread** quietly upstairs with Mum's surprise present.
The word is **tread**.

## Spelling test 7

**Spelling 1:** The word is **locks**.
Sam has two **locks** for his bike.
The word is **locks**.

**Spelling 2:** The word is **shoes**.
Maddie's mum bought her some new **shoes**.
The word is **shoes**.

**Spelling 3:** The word is **crying**.
My baby brother won't stop **crying**.
The word is **crying**.

**Spelling 4:** The word is **tunnel**.
The train went through a **tunnel**.
The word is **tunnel**.

**Spelling 5:** The word is **ear**.
Nishwa had a sore **ear**.
The word is **ear**.

**Spelling 6:** The word is **mixed**.
I **mixed** the eggs with the flour and sugar.
The word is **mixed**.

**Spelling 7:** The word is **phone**.
Mum used the **phone** to call Gran.
The word is **phone**.

**Spelling 8:** The word is **boys**.
The **boys** played with the girls.
The word is **boys**.

**Spelling 9:** The word is **donkey**.
The little **donkey** climbed up the hill.
The word is **donkey**.

**Spelling 10:** The word is **their**.
The children packed **their** bags for the trip.
The word is **their**.

## Spelling test 8

**Spelling 1:** The word is **all**.
Our teacher said we had **all** worked very hard.
The word is **all**.

**Spelling 2:** The word is **patted**.
Mike **patted** the dog gently.
The word is **patted**.

**Spelling 3:** The word is **wrong**.
I wrote down the **wrong** answer.
The word is **wrong**.

**Spelling 4:** The word is **huge**.
We climbed a **huge** tree in the garden.
The word is **huge**.

**Spelling 5:** The word is **paw**.
The cat had hurt its **paw**.
The word is **paw**.

# Spelling test transcripts

**Spelling 6:** The word is **toe**.
I banged my **toe** on the chair leg.
The word is **toe**.

**Spelling 7:** The word is **careless**.
Freddy could be quite **careless** with his belongings.
The word is **careless**.

**Spelling 8:** The word is **people**.
Some **people** are scared of dogs.
The word is **people**.

**Spelling 9:** The word is **everybody**.
I told **everybody** they could come to my party.
The word is **everybody**.

**Spelling 10:** The word is **national**.
We watched the **national** diving competition.
The word is **national**.

## Spelling test 9

**Spelling 1:** The word is **bottle**.
I filled my **bottle** with water.
The word is **bottle**.

**Spelling 2:** The word is **happier**.
Carla was much **happier** when she had learned her spellings.
The word is **happier**.

**Spelling 3:** The word is **shiny**.
Our teacher has a **shiny** new car.
The word is **shiny**.

**Spelling 4:** The word is **called**.
Alfie **called** his dog but it wouldn't come.
The word is **called**.

**Spelling 5:** The word is **hospital**.
We visited Gran in **hospital**.
The word is **hospital**.

**Spelling 6:** The word is **camel**.
A **camel** lives in the desert.
The word is **camel**.

**Spelling 7:** The word is **bare**.
In winter, the trees are **bare**.
The word is **bare**.

**Spelling 8:** The word is **clothes**.
Mum washed my dirty **clothes**.
The word is **clothes**.

**Spelling 9:** The word is **neatly**.
I can write my name **neatly**.
The word is **neatly**.

**Spelling 10:** The word is **world**.
We have been learning about places around the **world**.
The word is **world**.

## Spelling test 10

**Spelling 1:** The word is **buzz**.
I heard the bee **buzz** away.
The word is **buzz**.

**Spelling 2:** The word is **dry**.
The grass was **dry** so we sat down for our picnic.
The word is **dry**.

**Spelling 3:** The word is **time**.
It was **time** for lunch.
The word is **time**.

**Spelling 4:** The word is **knight**.
The **knight** rode a white horse.
The word is **knight**.

**Spelling 5:** The word is **tries**.
Millie **tries** hard to learn her times tables.
The word is **tries**.

**Spelling 6:** The word is **war**.
We learned what life was like in the **war**.
The word is **war**.

**Spelling 7:** The word is **water**.
Zainab spilled his drink of **water**.
The word is **water**.

**Spelling 8:** The word is **climb**.
It was a long **climb** up the hill.
The word is **climb**.

**Spelling 9:** The word is **quite**.
The cake wasn't **quite** cooked.
The word is **quite**.

**Spelling 10:** The word is **busy**.
We were **busy** practising for the school play.
The word is **busy**.

# Progress chart

Fill in your score in the table below to see how well you've done.

| Test number (Grammar, Punctuation and Spelling) | Score |
|---|---|
| Test 1 | |
| Test 2 | |
| Test 3 | |
| Test 4 | |
| Test 5 | |
| Test 6 | |
| Test 7 | |
| Test 8 | |
| Test 9 | |
| Test 10 | |
| **TOTAL** | |

| Mark | |
|---|---|
| **0–70** | Good try! You need more practice in some topics – ask an adult to help you. |
| **71–140** | You're doing really well. Ask for extra help for any topics you found tricky. |
| **141–200** | You're a 10-Minute SATs Test grammar, punctuation and spelling star – good work! |

GREAT WORK!

Well done!

*You have completed all of the 10-Minute SATs Tests*

Name: _____

Date: _____

# QUICK TESTS FOR SATs SUCCESS

## BOOST YOUR CHILD'S CONFIDENCE WITH 10-MINUTE SATs TESTS

- Bite-size mini SATs tests which take just 10 minutes to complete
- Covers key National Test topics
- Full answers and progress chart provided to track improvement
- Available for Years 2 and 6

**Find out more at www.scholastic.co.uk**